GUIDED

NEW YORK

readcereal.com

G

SAY HELLO

hello@readcereal.com

BE A STOCKIST

stockist@readcereal.com

ROSA PARK

Editor

RICH STAPLETON

Creative Director

RICHARD ASLAN

Sub Editor

JON RICH

Illustrator

Photography by **Matt Johnson, Kate Holstein, Justin Chung** & **Samantha Goh**

Words by **Kris Seto**

Published by Cereal Ltd.

Printed in the United Kingdom on FSC certified uncoated paper.

THE CONCEPT

We at *Cereal magazine* have travelled to cities around the world and sought out places that we believe to be unique, interesting, and enjoyable. Our aim is to produce guides that would befit Cereal readers and modern travellers alike, recommending a tightly edited selection of experiences that combine quality with meticulous design. If the food is top notch, so too is the space that accompanies it. You'll soon notice that our version of the perfect trip is woven in with an understated flair and a penchant for grand landscapes – both natural and manmade.

These guides complement what we do at *Cereal magazine*. Our print title is focussed on the timeless, the cultural, and the historical. We often discuss the language, local cuisine, architecture, and classic sights of a destination, so *GUIDED* is its welcome counterpart. Here you'll find the practical advice you need on where to stay, where to eat, what to see, and where to shop. Together, *Cereal* and *GUIDED* form the holistic approach to travel that we live by.

THE GUIDE

This guide to New York features a considered selection of shops, hotels, restaurants, cafes and points of interest. Not intended to be comprehensive, we present a discerning edit of our favourite places to visit in the city.

All photographs and copy are original and exclusive to Cereal.

TABLE OF CONTENTS

USA   JFK / LGA   ENGLISH   USD   +1

NEW YORK

S cott Fitzgerald found "wild promise of all the mystery and beauty in the world" here. Angela Carter believed "cities have sexes: London is a man, Paris is a woman, and New York is a well-adjusted transsexual." Simone de Beauvoir confided "there is something in New York air that makes sleep useless." Words are never enough for this city, so often evoked that even a first visit entails almost constant déjà-vu. This quintessential urban jungle delights us and tests us in equal measure; "In New York," as Charles Bukowski reminded us, "you've got to have all the luck."

ESSAYS: *My New York*

Fabrice Penot

Co-founder | LE LABO

I waited a long time for my first visit to New York City. I was 27. Within a year, my bags were packed to return. 12 months, I thought, would be long enough to get it out of my system and get back to my life in Paris. That was 12 years ago; I never left. Growing up in Châteauroux, a small town in the heart of France, few places seemed more remote than New York, but even then, something inside me told me I belonged here. Everything was strange at first, erratic and impatient. There was so much light, energy, and power that I was afraid to sleep in case I missed something. In Paris, I had been as grey and doubtful as the weather, but now, the permanent chaos matched what I had going on inside me; an energy that had always seemed too big for my body. New York was a game-changer, a rebirth. I found my geography of home.

This city isn't for everyone. It's a tough life and there are things I would change in a heartbeat; the subway, the garbage trucks, the frosty welcome at JFK after waiting in line for hours. Our interns arrive here from all over the world and within two weeks the city has adopted them. They know more people here than they ever knew back home. Depth – in love and friendship – must come quickly here. You find someone, but then you have to let them go again with a moment's notice. I still find it painful. But whenever my girlfriend and I talk about leaving (if you're sane, you have to ask the question during a New York winter) we come to the same conclusion and surrender to the knowledge that we'd miss it too much. They say New York makes you hate to love it, and sometimes I hate loving it so much that I realise I'm stuck. If I ever leave, I can never look back. It's like a love affair that made me happy beyond my wildest dreams. There might be others, but I know the best would be behind me.

This city is changing. I'm lucky enough that I won't be pushed out by exorbitant real estate prices, but there are days I worry I might be pushed out culturally and spiritually by a city I don't belong to any more. Living in Brooklyn protects us from the nonsense of Soho where we have our offices, but sometimes it feels like every cool little restaurant, store, or deli is being squeezed out of its lease, that the city is being bought out, bit by bit, with glass towers and millionaire apartments, generic brands replacing indie ones, streets turning into malls. If this city becomes some kind of Dubai-in-the-snow, then an unimaginable beauty will be lost. This is a city of doers, builders, and dreamers – and the size of your dream matters more than the size of your trust fund. If you don't have a dream waiting to be built, whoever you are, you don't belong here. This city was built by men in jeans and we New Yorkers are not ready to have it destroyed by men in suits. Despite the crazy money washing around and the bland apartments for rich kids to study and party in before returning home to London, São Paulo, or Hong Kong, the New York spirit lives on. You see it on the subway where everyone is fighting for survival. We could have a softer life anywhere else, but we get up with a sense of purpose; there is nowhere else we want to be.

I go to Tokyo, the Middle East, Russia, or Australia and see people buying our creations because they want a piece of this city. We have achieved something here. We didn't only survive but thrived, and that's amazing. I often cross the Brooklyn Bridge early in the morning on my way into work downtown, and it's breathtaking. I stop by at Café Colombe on Lafayette and Prince for my daily intake of caffeine. It's a tiny place which doesn't try too hard – you can't even really sit down – but it's an important part of my life. It's like the first 28 years of my life were preparation for all this. Everything I have ever built, I built here.

lelabofragrances.com

I n New York, like any city, it is necessary to find a niche, a place
where you fit. I was lucky enough to get a glimpse of what would
become my place on my very first trip here in 1985. I was enrolled
at the Royal Academy of Fine Arts in Arnhem, the Netherlands, and a
fellow student and I were invited here to put on a fashion show at the
famous new wave club, Danceteria. I have a memory of us holed up in
a basement on St. Mark's Place putting together the looks for the show,
surrounded by all that energy and vibrancy, having the time of our lives.

I had a feeling that I could live in the city immediately. It's easy to walk
around and get around. And the people are friendly. New Yorkers are
sometimes scolded for being shallow, but I haven't encountered very
much of that. A New Yorker will tell you his or her life story minutes
after meeting you. That's rare. In many ways, the city felt very much
like Amsterdam – where I grew up – with the liberal attitude, and the
melting pot of different cultures all gathered together in close quarters.
I felt welcomed. Plus, I got to take home a matchbook from Danceteria
and show my friends where I had been. I was thrilled.

Since moving here full time in 1994, I've lived in several
neighbourhoods: Brooklyn Heights, with its beautiful views of
downtown Manhattan and the bridges, the soaring Upper West Side,
and the Meatpacking District, where I was able to walk to work and stop
for a quiet breakfast along the way – a real luxury that living in the city
affords you.

But Williamsburg, where I've lived since 2010, reminds me most of
my first exciting moments in New York. There's so much going on, and

so much energy. Coffee shops, restaurants, workshops, record stores; something new is always opening up. When I visited New York as a young man, I always felt a jolt when I left that didn't subside for months. Now, I get that feeling every morning – I look left as I exit my building and see the skyline; it never fails. New York offers each of its citizens anonymity, and I love it for that. One of my favourite things to do is walk my Vizsla, Dutch, and simply observe - a fly on the wall, of sorts. I stroll down to the water, on North 9th Street and Kent, where there are soccer fields and the kids are out playing with their coaches. The most beautiful sunsets take place in Williamsburg, and crowds gather on the wooden benches, watching silently. It's so quiet in the evenings you can hear the traffic from Manhattan across the East River.

Williamsburg is known for being a party place on the weekends, but during the weekdays, it's quite intimate. The barista knows my order (a New Orleans style coffee at Blue Bottle on Berry Street; very lethal), and the *maître d'* at Aurora, the Italian restaurant on Grand Street, remembers my friends and I each time we come in. There is an authenticity in my neighbourhood. A creative spirit. Even our J.Crew store on Wythe Avenue has a completely different feel from the rest of our stores. We knew we had to keep as many of the original building elements as possible in order to retain a certain ambiance, or else it wouldn't work.

New Yorkers have their own language. In the Netherlands, we are very direct. I've had to learn to say things in a roundabout way here. If someone in New York says, "Oh, that's interesting," it means, "I don't like it at all!" It's more about what's not being said. And there's an art form to it. It's true that in New York there is always the opportunity to be surprised – by the people, by the weather, by something happening right outside your door that you never could have imagined.

I feel fortunate because New York has been so very kind to me. I feel rooted. I found my place. I feel more like a New Yorker now than a Dutchman. I'm wearing all denim! It's unavoidable if you live here really; you just become a part of it – operating in your own little space, but part of something so much larger.

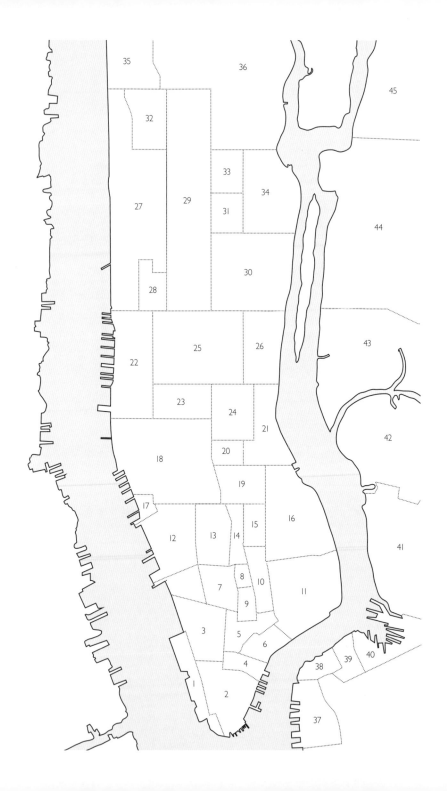

○ NEIGHBOURHOODS

1. Battery Park City
2. Financial District
3. Tribeca
4. Civic Center
5. Chinatown
6. Two Bridges
7. Soho
8. Nolita
9. Little Italy
10. Bowery
11. Lower East Side
12. West Village
13. Greenwich Village
14. Noho
15. East Village
16. Alphabet City
17. Meatpacking District
18. Chelsea
19. Gramercy
20. Nomad
21. Kips Bay
22. Hell's Kitchen
23. Garment District
24. Murray Hill
25. Midtown
26. Turtle Bay
27. Upper West Side
28. Lincoln Square
29. Central Park
30. Lenox Hill
31. Upper East Side
32. Manhattan Valley
33. Carnegie Hill
34. Yorkville
35. Morningside Heights
36. Harlem
37. Brooklyn Heights
38. DUMBO
39. Vinegar Hill
40. Navy Yard
41. Williamsburg
42. Greenpoint
43. Long Island City
44. Astoria
45. Steinway

PLACES TO GO

WYTHE HOTEL

Hotel

Old meets new at the Wythe Hotel, a 72 room boutique hotel settled into the walls of an old textile factory on the Williamsburg waterfront. Rich with Brooklyn flavour, it blends industrial details with local designs. The rooms are even stocked with artisanal snacks and small batch brews, should you want to sample the tastes of the neighbourhood without leaving your room. Visitors and guests can also dine at Reynard's for New American cuisine, or head up to The Ides, the Wythe's rooftop bar, to enjoy a cocktail as the sun sets.

📍 80 Wythe Ave, Brooklyn, NY 11249

⦿ Williamsburg

📞 718 460 8006

➤ wythehotel.com

THE NOLITAN
Hotel

Stay at The Nolitan and you'll quickly feel like a local. This 55 room boutique hotel is set amid residential Nolita and within walking distance of Soho, the Lower East Side, Chinatown, Little Italy, and the East Village, which puts you at the crossroads of cool. The hotel evokes a lived in feel with clean, masculine design details that conjure your own (albeit much more stylish) apartment. As part of their above-and-beyond amenities, you can even rent a bicycle, skateboard, video game system, or iPad for the duration of your stay.

📍 30 Kenmare St, New York, NY 10012

⭕ Nolita

📞 212 925 2555

↱ nolitanhotel.com

THE NOMAD
Hotel

Through The NoMad Hotel's dark, velvety entrance you'll discover an adult playground that brings together a Parisian aesthetic with a New York sensibility. The bar and restaurant is a maze of little rooms and nooks, each with its own vibe, charm, and cast of characters. Dine here and chef Daniel Humm and restaurateur Will Guidara, of Michelin three star rated Eleven Madison Park fame, will deliver an exceptional experience to remember.

📍 1170 Broadway, New York, NY 10001

⭕ Nomad

📞 212 796 1500

➡ thenomadhotel.com

MANDARIN ORIENTAL
Hotel

The view of Central Park and the Manhattan skyline from the Mandarin Oriental is worth the room rate alone. It's a stunning bird's eye view of an iconic city, and one of the reasons why the hotel is so special. Each of its rooms and suites, which start at the 35th floor, have floor to ceiling windows with views out across the New York.

80 Columbus Circle, New York, NY 10023

Midtown

212 805 8800

mandarinoriental.com/newyork

SWEATSHOP
Cafe

Aussies Luke Woodard and Ryan De Remer have brought a taste of Melbourne stateside with this modern coffee shop, which also doubles as their workspace. Virtually every detail was conceived and created by the industrial and graphic design duo, from the custom shelves to the communal table and benches, as well as the socks, hats, and apparel available for purchase. Their ethos is simple; serve great coffee, great design, and great food.

232 Metropolitan Ave, Brooklyn, NY 11211

Williamsburg

646 388 2483

sweatshop.nyc

LONG BLACK [americano]	3
SHORT MAC [macchiato]	3²⁵
PICCOLO	3⁵⁰
LONG MAC [cortado]	3⁵⁰
FLAT WHITE	4
CAP	4
LATTE	4
[extras: soy, almond, iced]	+50c
[chai, single origin]	+1
DRIP	2⁵⁰
COLDIE [iced coffee]	3⁷⁵
AUSSIE ICED COFFEE	5⁵⁰
TEA / HOT CHOC	3⁵⁰
JAFFLE [grilled cheese]	4
[add ham, baked beans]	+1⁵⁰
[add vegemite]	+1

AP CAFE

Cafe & Restaurant

After exploring the street art of Bushwick, visit AP Cafe to grab a coffee, light fare, or weekend brunch, and channel your own creativity. The airy, minimalist space is the perfect place to let your mind wander or get some work done. With plenty of natural light, succulent greenery, and a dreamy chillout soundtrack, your best ideas will flow effortlessly.

420 Troutman St, Brooklyn, NY 11237

Bushwick

347 404 6147

apcafenyc.com

HAPPY BONES
Cafe

This Nolitan coffee shop is the perfect pit stop after a day of Soho shopping. Expect great coffee, great vibes and even some local art for extra flavour. The cafe composts, only buys fair trade Counter Culture Coffee, and donates a part of their profits to Free Arts NYC, a nonprofit that brings educational arts and mentoring programmes to underserved children and families. So you can drink good coffee and do good at the same time.

394 Broome St, New York, NY 10013

Nolita

212 673 3754

happybonesnyc.com

HAPPY BONES

COFFEE
NEW YORK CITY

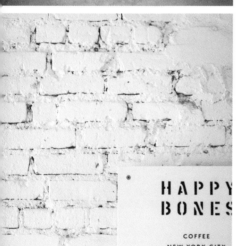

HAPPY BONES

COFFEE
NEW YORK CITY

Filter Coffee: 2 / 2.5
Espresso, Americano: 3 /
Macchiato, Piccolo: 3
Cortado: 3.75
Cappuccino, Flat White
Latte, Iced Latte: 4.5
Iced Coffee: 4.0
Hot Chocolate: 4.0
Bellocq Teas: 3.5
Extras: 0.5

NALATA NALATA

Homewares

There's something poetic about holding an object that has been designed and crafted to the point of perfection. You can feel the painstaking care, thought, and discipline that have been poured into it. At Nalata Nalata, you can also learn about its history. With a focus on the artists and how each item is made, storeowners Stevenson Aung and Angélique Chmielewski have assembled a collection of their favourite functional objects from around the world. Expect exceptional items for living, lounging, storing, cooking, and more.

2 Extra Pl, New York, NY 10003

Bowery

212 228 1030

nalatanalata.com

STILL HOUSE

Homewares & Accessories

P art gift shop, part home shop, and full of hidden wonders, Still House is a small boutique located in the East Village stocking a variety of charming just-offbeat-enough *tchotchkes*, including geometric jewellery, statement vases, handmade cards, Japanese ceramics, tabletop décor, and more. Shop owner Urte Tylaite curates a diverse collection of treasures from local and international artists. Leave plenty of time to explore every corner.

117 E 7th St, New York, NY 10009

East Village

212 539 0200

stillhousenyc.com

STEVEN ALAN HOME

Homewares & Accessories

Steven Alan brings his keen curatorial eye to his Tribeca outpost designed for domestic affairs. The spare, skylit space has a stylish, worldly air, housing an eclectic array of home goods, furniture, and linens, all discovered by Steven. The collection, which rotates regularly, includes a varied mix of ceramics, dinnerware, candles, and vintage one-of-a-kind lamps.

📍 158 Franklin St, New York, NY 10013

⭕ Tribeca

📞 646 402 9661

➜ stevenalan.com/home

THE APARTMENT BY THE LINE

Lifestyle Store

D esigned to feel like a real, lived in Soho loft, The Apartment by The Line is the online retailer's intimate showroom and living embodiment of the home and lifestyle brand. Every item in the apartment is available for purchase, including the artwork, clothing and accessories, and furniture – even the espresso machine is up for grabs. The knowledgeable guides will help you learn more about the ideas, traditions, and materials behind each item, and inspire you to embark on your own interior design endeavours.

📍 76 Greene St, 3rd Floor, New York, NY 10012

⭕ Soho

📞 646 678 4908

➤ theline.com

LA GARÇONNE

Womenswear

This elegant online retailer has moved into a bricks and mortar home in Tribeca; a Japanese inspired, white walled space to fit their minimalist aesthetic. Shop for the best in luxurious, understated womenswear and lifestyle brands, including The Row, Maison Margiela, La Garçonne Moderne and J.W. Anderson.

📍 465 Greenwich St, New York, NY 10013

⭕ Tribeca

📞 646 553 3303

➦ lagarconne.com

C'H'C'M'

Menswear

Sweetu Patel has created a temple to true modern menswear at this Noho boutique. The shop carries its own namesake brand alongside special collaboration projects and a changing roster of select, easy to wear but hard to find international labels. There's a purity to every garment – a weightiness that can be seen in the cut, materials, and impeccable detailing. Drop in regularly to catch the rotating artwork, events, and pop-up shop additions.

📍 2 Bond St, New York, NY, 10012

⭕ Noho

📞 212 673 8601

➡ chcmshop.com

UNIS

Menswear

Simple and understated, UNIS is an ideal place to find timeless wardrobe classics such as the perfect pant, the cardigan you'll wear year round, or the laid back, lived in t-shirt. Despite its cult following, not an ounce of pretence is present in the Nolita store. Alongside their own brand, UNIS also stocks favourites including Haerfest, Common Projects, and Malin + Goetz. It's a must visit for men looking for stylish, well tailored basics.

226 Elizabeth St, New York, NY 10012

Nolita

212 431 5533

unisnewyork.com

DASHWOOD BOOKS

Bookshop

Where do the world's most influential photographers and creatives go to find inspiration? This Bond Street basement shop is a dedicated homage to the image and image makers, specialising in rare and out of print photography books. You can find independently published gems that cover preeminent photographers and their work from the 1950s to the present day.

33 Bond St, New York, NY 10012

Noho

212 387 8520

dashwoodbooks.com

MCNALLY JACKSON

Bookshop

Stumble into Sarah McNally's two storey bookshop and you may never leave. The independent icon has a 20 seat teahouse for you to wind down and explore their comprehensive selection of 55,000 volumes and 8,300 title literature collection, all organised by geographical region. Their well read staff can help you find exactly what you're looking for, or help you unearth something entirely novel. Check the calendar for author readings or workshops taking place during your visit.

52 Prince St, New York, NY 10012

Nolita

212 274 1160

mcnallyjackson.com

DIMES

Restaurant

There is a comfort food rule of thumb; eating out of a bowl makes everything taste better. Given how addictive the food at Dimes is, there must be some truth to it. This easygoing eatery focusses on health conscious, earthy Californian style cuisine. Picture simple, superfood ingredients, such as kale, coconut milk, beets, brussel sprouts, quinoa, açaí, and salmon combined in imaginative, unexpected ways, and bursting with flavour.

📍 49 Canal St, New York, NY 10002

⭕ Lower East Side

📞 212 925 1300

➡ dimesnyc.com

FIVE LEAVES

Restaurant

Travel to the Greenpoint side of McCarren Park on any given weekend, and you are likely to find a small gathering of salivating brunchers waiting their turn to sink their teeth into the incredible offering at this chilled Aussie influenced New American bistro. Try the signature burger, truffle fries, or ricotta pancakes. Equally appetising is the vintage nautical décor.

18 Bedford Ave, Brooklyn, NY 11222

Greenpoint

718 383 5345

fiveleavesny.com

EGG SHOP

Restaurant

A s the name suggests, it's all about the incredible, edible, and demonstratively versatile egg. At this sunny Nolita restaurant, you can choose from a number of creative and comforting dishes including the Egg Salad Sandwich (add the fried chicken), El Camino (a poached egg topping pulled pork carnitas and avocado), and the classic Benedict. It's a bright, bustling joint that gets especially busy at the weekend. Arrive early. The early bird gets the egg.

📍 151 Elizabeth St, New York, NY, 10012

⭘ Nolita

📞 646 666 0810

↪ eggshopnyc.com

EN JAPANESE BRASSERIE

Restaurant

Amid the many upscale Japanese establishments in the West Village, EN Japanese Brasserie stands out thanks to its striking interior, Japanese *izakaya* spirit, and seasonal cuisine honouring the flavour of every ingredient. *Sake* and *shōchū* lovers will rejoice at the extensive selection. Be sure to order the housemade tofu, a must eat treat.

435 Hudson St, New York, NY 10014

West Village

212 647 9196

enjb.com

LOCANDA VERDE

Restaurant

After a morning of wandering Tribeca's picturesque streets, head over to Locanda Verde for lunch, and feast on chef Andrew Carmellini's soulful Italian food. Choose a few of their *cicchetti* (snacks) to share and relish in the restaurant's bustling atmosphere, evocative of a gentleman's club, accented by tufted leather seats, wooden tables, and brass finishes. Wine and spirit connoisseurs will enjoy the extensive drink menu.

📍 377 Greenwich St, New York, NY 10013

⭕ Tribeca

📞 212 925 3797

↪ locandaverdenyc.com

MAIALINO

Restaurant

Located in the Gramercy Park Hotel, Maialino is one of our favourite spots in the city. This warm and inviting restaurant evokes a Roman trattoria with a standing barista station, a sweets and pastry front, and a bustling bar, each of which breathe a unique energy into the space. Executive chef Nick Anderer serves a rustic Italian menu that's top notch. You can't go wrong with anything on the menu, but the ricotta pancakes with pear compote holds a sweet spot in our hearts (and bellies).

2 Lexington Ave, New York, NY 10010

Gramercy

212 777 2410

maialinonyc.com

THE MORGAN LIBRARY & MUSEUM
Museum

Tucked into Manhattan's Murray Hill neighbourhood, this literature lover's oasis was originally founded in 1906, to house the private library of financier J.P. Morgan. The museum is filled with rich relics, original manuscripts, rare prints, mediaeval artworks, and historical drawings from Leonardo, Michelangelo, Raphael, and Rembrandt. View J.D. Salinger's letters, soak in Edgar Allen Poe's phantasmagorical world, and admire the three ancient Gutenberg Bibles in this beautiful Palladian space.

225 Madison Ave, New York, NY 10016

Murray Hill

212 685 0008

themorgan.org

THE NOGUCHI MUSEUM
Museum

An overwhelming sense of peace descends whenever you enter The Noguchi Museum. The immaculate space, designed by the influential artist and sculptor himself, showcases a wide range of his work including monumental stone sculptures, landscape architecture, furniture design, and photography. It's the embodiment of Noguchi's philosophy; a focus on surface, space, and the utmost respect for his materials.

9-01 33rd Rd, Queens, NY 11106

Astoria

718 204 7088

noguchi.org

ADDITIONAL RECOMMENDATIONS

ABC COCINA | *Restaurant*

ACME | *Restaurant & Bar*

BELLOCQ TEA ATELIER | *Cafe*

THE FAT RADISH | *Restaurant*

THE HIGH LINE | *Park*

HOTEL AMERICANO | *Hotel*

IL BUCO ALIMENTARI & VINERIA | *Restaurant*

MORGENSTERN'S FINEST ICE CREAM | *Ice Cream Parlour*

NEUE GALERIE | *Museum*

NEW YORK PUBLIC LIBRARY | *Library & Museum*

SHUKO | *Restaurant*

SATURDAYS SURF | *Shop & Cafe*

TOBY'S ESTATE | *Cafe*

CEREAL

TRAVEL & STYLE